ISBN - Paperback 978-1-8380196-6-2 | eBook 978-1-8380196-7-9

Sea Salt Publishing
Bournemouth, Dorset, UK

Websites:

www.seasaltlearning.com

www.julianstodd.wordpress.com

Power

And Potential

CONTENTS

INTRODUCTION

To be a leader is to hold power, but the type of power that you hold, and where you hold it, is not set in stone.

Some power may be held structurally, within the hierarchy, given to you by the Organisation you work for, and arranged into rules, systems, process, and mechanisms of consequence and control.

Other types of power are unwritten, held within our reputation in the community, or through the influence, or coercion, that comes from seniority or expertise, stories, or beliefs.

Power is complex: it is not a one-dimensional force, but a multidimensional one. Sometimes the different forms of power that we hold in these different dimensions can operate against one another, while at other times they can be mutually exclusive. For example, you may fail to be authentic in your own beliefs and concurrently obedient within a formal system.

Whatever type of power we are discussing, whatever form of leadership we think we need, three things are always true.

- Firstly, all power has limits. We may not realise it, we may never probe it, but power always has an edge. Understanding the limits of our power may be more important than understanding the substance of it.

- Secondly, all power can be opposed. However powerful we feel, and however all-encompassing the extent of our control feels, power can always be opposed. That is, at least by those willing to pay the price.

- Thirdly, and finally, all power has a cost, both to ourselves, and to others. Nothing is free: it may demand our consensus or obedience, our freedom or virtue, our followership or sacrifice.

To be a leader in the Social Age is to understand this, and to embrace it; to learn our limits and build our portfolio of powers; to consider how the story of our leadership (and the story of our Organisation) evolves, and to think how those stories are amplified; and to be aware of the price we must pay, or are demanding from others.

In The Social Leadership Handbook, I outlined the premise that we hold power in both formal and social systems, and that a modern Socially Dynamic Organisation may need us to lead in both – or, more specifically, at the intersection of the two.

In this book, using a simple Enquiry Framework, we will consider the shape of power that we hold, and the potential that this gives us.

AN ENQUIRY FRAMEWORK

This book is not an instruction manual, nor an answer. It's an Enquiry Framework: a set of related questions that provide scaffolding - or form a space - for us to explore the nature, operation, and shape of our power.

We will explore our power as Social Leaders through four different lenses.

1   We will consider the mechanisms of our power and how we are powerful.

2   We will explore the shape of our power and consider how we find the edges.

3   We will seek to understand the impact of our power and where consequences lie.

4   We will discover the fragility of our power and how this humility may make us stronger.

You may look at these questions in the order written here, or in any order you choose. While they do not rely on each other, some sections reference others for brevity or ease.

I have written the book to follow the format of the four-week programme entitled 'Social Leadership: Power and Potential', but it will work perfectly well standing alone.

Alternatively, you could form a book club, or lunch group, to share the questions and journey with.

As you read these questions, I would encourage you to step out of your comfort zone. Try not to reinforce what you already know and feel, but rather explore the vulnerable edges.

Be unafraid to be curious, to explore, and to be wrong.

This is not just a book, but a book about power. It will potentially help you find your own.

If we understand our power, we may gain some insight into our own potential: not the space we currently inhabit, but the space we may earn.

There are no universal answers. The journey itself is what we will take away, and those whom we meet in the process

IMPERFECTION AND GRAFFITI

As ever with my work, it's adaptive and evolutionary, which is another way of saying imperfect and sometimes wrong.

GRAFFITI
SPACE

I would encourage you to expand on it, and adapt it to your own situation. Indeed, you may want to graffiti this book with your own questions and ideas, before handing it on to someone else.

Enquiry frameworks are great for hearing diverse stories, but terrible for uncovering 'one truth'. Fortunately, I do not believe that an exploration of our power as leaders requires 'one truth'; rather, it requires individual truth.

Use this book, this structure, as a tool. Consider it as scaffolding surrounding the space in which you are searching.

THE MECHANISMS OF YOUR POWER

In this first section, we will be considering your power and where the edges of it lie.

We will consider: what you can achieve alone?, how you influence others?, what lies beyond your control?, and how your power is limited?

These are not the only four questions that we could ask, but they will help to guide us through how your power works.

Using these questions during our enquiry, we should take things that we are certain of and break them apart.

There is nothing special about the questions I have written. If you prefer, you can use your own questions. The most important thing is to start with areas of certainty, and to avoid gazing into the distance.

© Julian St.

1.

WHAT CAN YOU ACHIEVE, ALONE?

Consider what you can achieve alone.

Entirely alone.

Can you dig a hole?

Can you drive to work?

Can you cook a meal?

Even these things come with a reliance on others. For example, a spade is forged by someone else, your car runs smoothly because a mechanic trained well, and the right recipes are often shared by third parties.

We are social creatures at heart, which means more than simply being conversational. We live in interdependent systems and co-dependent relationships, which, whilst overlaid with marketplaces and rituals, are ultimately what make us similar.

We often feel we are acting with agency, but it's worth considering how that agency is found: often it is through the permission, support, hard work, or consensus of others.

To understand this, the relationship between 'self' and 'system' must be acknowledged as important. It allows us to take action.

Perhaps there is a difference between the terms 'solitary' and 'alone'. Thinking can be a 'solitary', as well as a collaborative, activity: but do we do it 'alone'?

My thinking is influenced: by my reading, by my communities, by my beliefs. It does not take place in isolation, but rather entirely within certain contexts. It is not truly 'alone', although it is often 'solitary'.

The colours that I paint my thinking in are part of a broader palette, if you like.

Organisations are inherently collective. However, they may require work to be synergistic and effective.

To be part of an Organisation implies a whole. Therefore, our power is intrinsically nested within a structure.

There are undoubtedly things that we do alone, but often these are within a broader sequence of activities that are collective or collaborative, or dependent upon the actions or goodwill of others.

Understanding the collective nature of much of our power – either through the ways it is granted or how it is moderated – can lead us to view power as more of a collective than an individual phenomenon. This in turn can guide our actions.

- Is it always clear what sequence an action lies within?

- Is it possible that parts of a sequence are hidden from us?

- Do we sometimes feel we have achieved 'alone' simply because we are blind to the input of, or our dependence on, others?

- Are you more satisfied with solitary achievement than teamwork?

- Are some things simply impossible together, or conversely impossible alone?

2.

WHAT CAN YOU INFLUENCE OTHERS TO DO?

If only part of our power is 'alone', then do we understand how we bend others to our will?

- If effectiveness is a collective effort, who sets the direction, and who steers the ship? And how?

Consider what you are able to influence others to do, and the ways in which you do so. Do you paint pictures or incite action?

Consider what you can influence others to do. Can you influence them simply to take blind action, or to think differently about the actions that they take?

- Do you push or pull?

Influence may be about handing over directions and a story, or supporting people in finding their own. It may be overt or implicit. Benign or toxic.

We should recognise that influence is not simply an activity: it is a feature of the context in which our leadership is held.

Simply being called a 'leader' in a formal system provides context and may influence others directly.

Similarly, being called a 'troublemaker' provides context and may influence others too.

Particularly, it may influence others to oppose you, or join you. Hence, a study of power is linked to a study of social movements more generally, seen as sequences of storytelling and a mobilisation of power.

- Can you achieve consistency across a team, or does your influence cause divergence, or even disagreement or polarity? Is that, too, contextual?

- Is your influence like a penknife that can be used to carry out many tasks? Or like a hammer, which does one thing well and may cause damage if used incorrectly?

- Is your influence held within a reputation, a personal story, your charisma, or something else?

- Is influence always a conscious act, or can people be influenced by you even when you don't want them to be? If so, should you carry any responsibility (or should you be rewarded) for their actions?

3.

WHAT OUTCOMES ARE BEYOND YOUR CONTROL?

Some things will forever remain beyond our control, while others may come within our control if we make changes.

To understand what lies beyond our control may help us to conceive and drive change, or conversely it may help us to find peace within our limitations.

Some things that are beyond our control are obvious: you may not be able to set a budget, change a rule, or protect yourself from oversight. You may be unable to lift a weight, convince a person, or deliver on time. You may be unable to get to sleep or wake up on demand.

Some things are beyond your direct control, but may nevertheless lie within your sphere of influence.

The ways in which we exert our formal power are clear: we can push a button, make people fearful or reward them heavily, tell someone to do something, or create a system or process that dictates actions and responses.

However, some things cannot be dictated. I cannot create a system that will make you trust me; I cannot order or pay you to trust me either.

To understand 'control' is to understand which mechanism is relevant at any particular time, and to understand, when two mechanisms are available (e.g. direct order and influence), which is best.

Put simply, sometimes our power is best utilised by not being exerted at all. Instead of 'telling', we can simply create space and circumstance for agency.

This may depend upon the outcome we seek. If we desire a specific and unified course of action, we may need more of our formal, controlling power, as this type of power specialises in consistency, conformity, and replicability.

If, on the other hand, we are happy to arrive at an outcome via various routes (or indeed are happy with various outcomes), we may consider influence, facilitation, enablement, increments, iteration of action, or even rebellion.

In some ways, this leads to the broader question of 'what is the point of a leader?' Is a leader there to take action or to enable action to be taken?

- **Can you think of something that lies beyond your control?**

- **How do you feel about it?**

4.

WHAT LIMITS YOUR POWER?

I have said that all power has limits,
but what is it that limits your power?

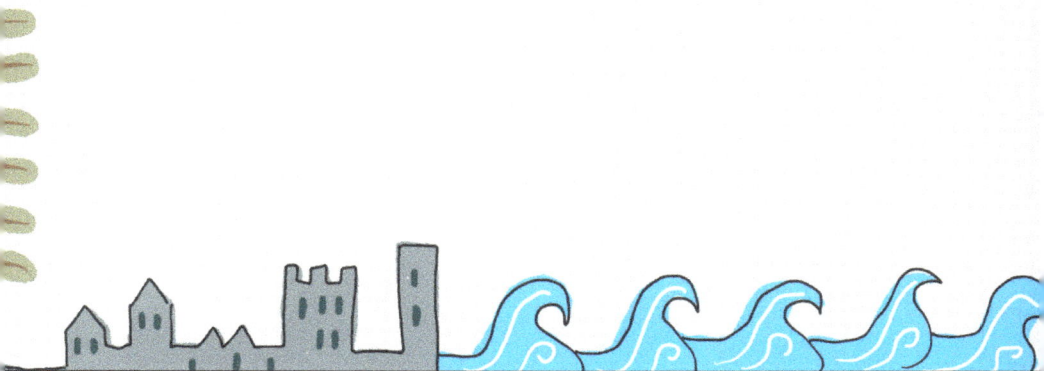

Within a formal system, the answer is often relatively easy to find. It could be your contract, terms of reference, organisational rules, or broader legal frameworks that limit your power.

Your contract determines interpersonal relationships and structures of power, as well as how consequences are controlled; it tells you whom you can order about, and whom you have to report to. Specific projects or instructions, of course, may vary the particulars.

More broadly, an Organisation may have macro rules or principles, for example pertaining to diversity, inclusion, or social responsibility, that also limit what you can do. Ultimately, we operate within regulatory and legal environments that control the limits of our power. We cannot fairly instruct someone to break the law, because the law limits our power to do so.

These things, however, do not define your power. Perhaps we can better view them as defining the box, or space, within which your power exists.

There are powerful secondary and tertiary layers of mechanisms – culture and normalisation – that define even our formal power.

Culture is a socially constructed layer of context, constraint, delusion, and interpretation around the formal rules. We can view culture as either the oil or the grit in the machine, although it may be hard to distinguish between the two. Sometimes it can be both, depending on the context.

Culture also manifestly limits our power, because certain actions can cross-culturally established mechanisms, and hence be opposed.

This may be simple, or complex, to see in action.

A common mistake is to imagine that we have 'one culture'. The truth is that we simply don't. Culture is a story told many times; the interpretation and understanding that we hold in our heads is the one that we most often act upon.

Perhaps it is better to see culture as a collection of broadly shared narratives, held within divergent, individual stories.

Normalisation is broader than culture, reflecting culturally normalised attitudes, even at societal level. Common assumptions about the role of mothers would be an example, or the wisdom of age.

Normalised features of culture limit us, being often so implicit that we fail to even see them. Hence we are limited, but blind to that limitation.

Of course, sometimes the limitation of our power is more direct. We are, for instance, limited by someone else who has more power than us, whether this power is in the same dimension or a superior one.

For example, you may be senior enough to make a decision and to take action, but if someone of a higher reputation, a perceived greater authenticity, and with more experience challenges you, then you may become limited and unable to succeed.

In other words, claimed power can limit granted power, in certain contexts.

I use that word a lot: context. This is because power is always held within a particular context.

- Think about the things that limit your power: which are obvious, and which are harder to identify?

- Which aspects of your power are limited: the things you can do socially, or those you can do formally?

- Which limitations are fixed, and which are contextual?

GRAFFITI SPACE

THE IMPACT OF YOUR POWER

In this second section, we consider the impact of your power.

We operate within fragile ecosystems (if you are particularly interested in the idea of the organisation as ecosystem, I spend a chapter exploring this in Quiet Leadership).

A Social Leader will explore the impact of any action, positive or not, to better understand the shelter that they provide or the shadows that they cast.

We will consider a further four questions in this section, including the good that you can do and the harm that you can prevent, how your power enables others, and how you calibrate your action by hearing your impact.and to avoid gazing into the distance.

5.

WHAT GOOD CAN YOU DO?

We veer into subjectivity here, as well as potential irrelevance. It may not be your goal to be good, nor your job. Yet the atmosphere in which a healthy Organisation operates must surely work towards the belief that there is a net benefit.

An Organisation that delivers profit at the cost of the mental and/or physical health of its employees, has major problems to deal with.

Consider what good you can do. With all your power, both formal and social, are you able to deliver good outcomes?

Really, we should start by asking what 'good' means, because (unsurprisingly) the notion of 'good' is contextual too.

If I am a shareholder, then a dividend may be 'good'.

However, if I am an employee, a pay rise or the creation of a new training opportunity, using that same money, may be 'good'.

This demonstrates that leadership can find itself stuck between 'self' and 'system'. For every action, we must actively consider context, or at least be aware that we operate within a context. 'Good' is not an absolute value.

- Within this understanding, what good can you do?

- Can you make one person's day better?

- Can you improve culture (alone, with others, or through others)?

- Can you help in every, or any, context?

- What types of problem can you solve? What types of problem are always beyond you?

You could reasonably challenge the question. Perhaps, for instance, you feel that all your actions are good. I certainly feel that most of mine are. I rarely set out to be harmful, although perhaps my actions sometimes inadvertently cause harm, beyond my sight.

To ask what good you can do is a mindful activity. We may not be able to answer the question directly, but perhaps the act of looking itself is enough.

If you find yourself desiring to do good, but can't be specific, perhaps that in itself is useful to understand.

6.

WHAT HARM CAN YOU PREVENT?

Related to our first question (and perhaps the flip side of the coin), we can ask ourselves: what harm we can prevent?

- With all the power vested in you by your communities, and granted to you by your Organisation, what harm can you prevent (and how)?

Perhaps there are two aspects to consider: one is about specific intervention, and the other is more cultural.

- Does your leadership create, or support, a culture in which harm is less likely,

- Are you able to spot, diagnose, or hear of instances where direct action is necessary?

In an earlier work on Social Leadership, I wrote that 'Social Leaders do what is right, not simply what is easy', which was a rather trite thing to say. Most of us, of course, seek to do what is right, although all too often we stick to what is easy.

But trite as it may be, the question is valid: do you do what is right, or what is easy? And when seeking to prevent harm, do you always take the easy or the hard path, or is it... wait for it... contextual?!

At the sharpest edge of this space, the real question is whether you are willing to stand up and be counted. If you see something wrong, are you prepared to challenge it, or is your willingness dependent upon the price of action?

I always remember a friend telling me, as she went through a constructive dismissal process, that a fellow executive member of the board 'stood alongside her', and 'told her that what was happening was wrong' – but never acted to prevent harm. While he had awareness, and intent, crucially he had no willingness.

I can easily blame him for that, and of course the price is paid not only by individuals, but by their families too. Losing a job, or losing influence and reputation, has a real cost.

Sometimes, despite this, you have to stand up.

At a broader, cultural level, the question we must ask is how the culture formed in the first place.

- What is the connection between leadership and culture? Does a leader 'set the tone', or simply give the space? Does a leader pollute and/or colour the culture, like a drop of ink in water? Do they dictate it?

- Is the role of a leader to always prevent harm?

Could a leader's role, conceivably, be to sometimes 'do' harm? What about through competition? Is 'harm' the inevitable flip side of 'good'? Does the coin always have both faces?

7.

HOW DO YOU ENABLE?

It may go without saying that leaders 'enable', but how exactly? And is that a leader's core purpose, or a means to an end?

GRAFFITI SPACE

- Do you give instructions, resources, or space? Do you rely on process or intuition?

- Do you measure the effectiveness of your enabling actions, or assume you are always brilliant?

- Is your enablement spread equally, or are you more likely to enable those who you like or need, or those who are most likely to succeed or be obedient?

- Do you ever enable people who oppose you? Or does your very opposition enable them in some way?

8.

HOW DO YOU HEAR IMPACT FROM YOUR ACTIONS?

Every action that we take has an impact, part of which we can hear, and part of which may be out of earshot.

Use this question to consider what you are hearing, and how much of the story that forms.

Our inability to hear may be down to dulled hearing, the fact that we are standing too far away, or the fact that we are being whispered about behind our backs.

Some stories we miss because they are quiet, others because they are hidden.

Impact is feedback: it can make us feel better or make us feel annoyed. Both these things can loop back to change our action, to incite us to go further, or to drive us into shelter and retreat.

- To what lengths do you go to hear the impact?

- Do you observe, do you ask people, or do you infer from their behaviour and actions over time?

- Do you just guess?

- Do you hear impact in the everyday, or does special time need to be set aside?

- Will feedback on impact be forthcoming in every instance, or is there groundwork to do in order to earn the right to hear it?

- Do people need to trust you to give you feedback on impact? Or, conversely, should they just be annoyed at you?

In Quiet Leadership, I talk about 'intention', 'action', and 'impact'. In short, we have the intention to act, we take action, and it has an impact. These steps, however, do not always come together seamlessly. I may have good intent, take action that I believe to be good, and hope for good impact, but that does not make it so.

Often our action is diluted or polluted: for example, my intention may be pure, my action tempered by circumstance, and my impact consequently dulled.

In Quiet Leadership, I also talk about how we all cast shadows, even the best of us, under the best of circumstances. If we operate in the sun, we cast a shadow. This leads us to question whether we are looking into the light, or behind us at the dark.

- How would we ever see our impact if it lies in the dark? Would it be through our own eyes, or through the eyes of others?

THE SHAPE OF YOUR POWER

In this third section, we will explore the Shape of your Power. We will consider four questions: where your power sits?, where the edges lie?, what you have been given?, and what you can demand?

All power has limits, in terms of its reach and legitimacy. All power, likewise, has edges, with the shape of my power being different to yours. To have an understanding of the shape of our individual power, as well as that of others, may help us plan for development, and also for complementary strength.

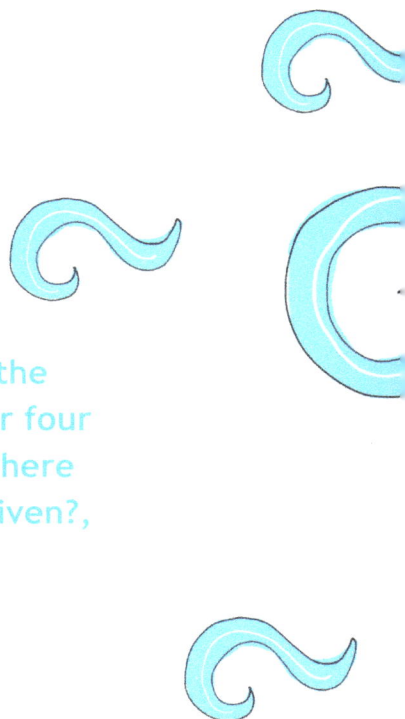

©Julian Stodd

9.

WHERE DOES YOUR POWER SIT?

Like buildings, all power has its foundations: in your contract, your role, your reputation, your story, or in many other places besides.

One of the ways in which we gain power is by getting a new job, or taking on a new responsibility, through a formal system. Simply taking on a new project may bring with it more power.

Sharing can be another foundation for power. If you are a great curator of content, or editor of the obscure, you may find power with a foundation in this skill. Can you write coherently about blockchain for the masses? There's power in that. Can you cut through complexity? There's power in that too.

Another way is to gain newfound knowledge or expertise, especially knowledge or expertise that is rare or particularly in demand. Simply knowing how to use a bit of software well may create power, or having the ability to advise others on which software to buy.

Your power may sit in a formal space, a social one, or both. Indeed, Social Leadership itself is a type of power that sits in both – beyond formal mandate, with social authority.

Formal power is not limitless, but it is subdivisible. We can always split responsibilities down, narrowing scope or giving depth.

Social power may actually be harder to divide. While I can note your reputation, I cannot guarantee it or gift it.

- Does your power operate universally, or only once you walk through the doors (or enter the Teams call) at work?

- Does your power persist unchanged over time, or fade with a passing project or role? Does it operate globally, or just in your office or household?

- Does everyone experience your power the same way, or are team members treated differently to fellow employees beyond your team?

- Do people even know you have power, and how?

- How much of your power travels with you, like luggage, and how much stays still, like the hotel?

10.

WHERE ARE YOU POWERLESS?

If all power has limits, then it stands to reason that some people are powerless all of the time, or that we are all powerless some of the time.

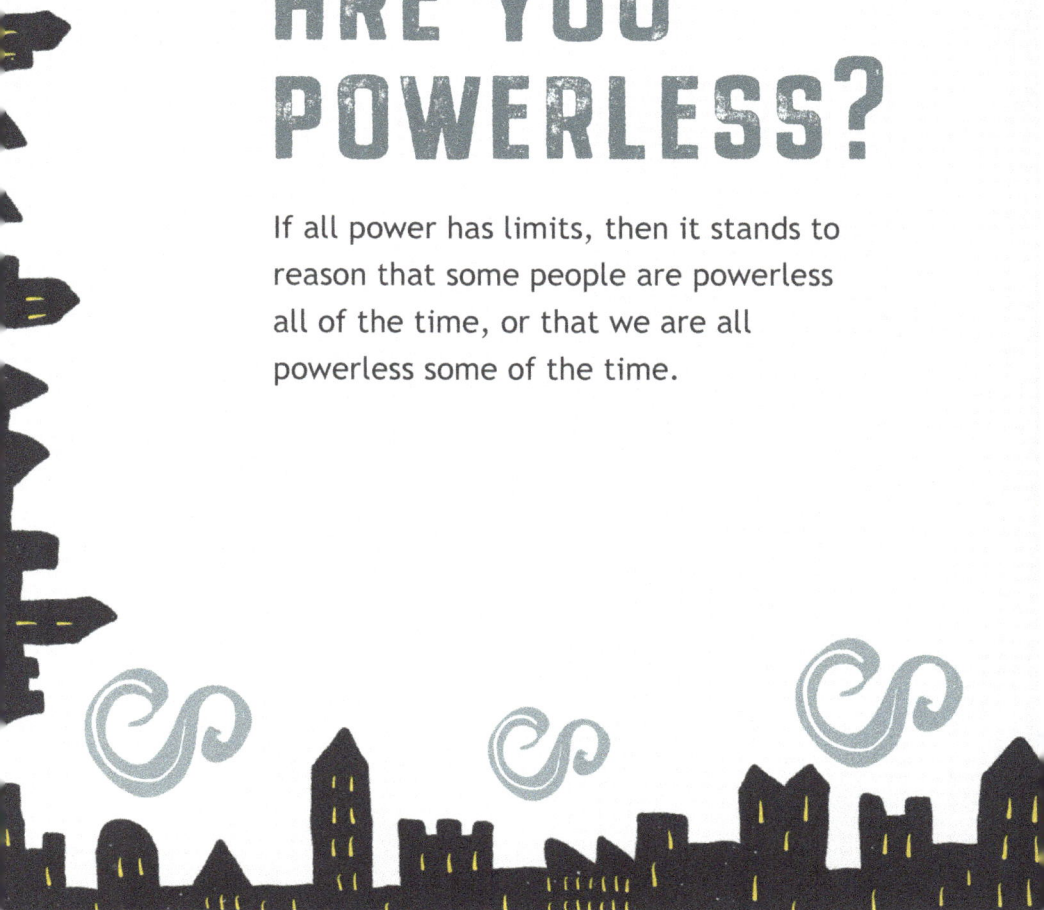

Nobody can be all-powerful, if only because some types of power can only be held in opposition, and you cannot (easily) oppose yourself.

Of course, you can change your position and view over time, which may itself bring you power, or cause you to lose it.

> • **When you are powerless, is that because you lack enough power, you are outclassed, your power is degraded, or because you simply have none?**

Sometimes we may find that we are powerful in certain contexts, but that we are powerless to set the context. Or, conversely, we may find that we hold power, but that other people are able to evade or outclass it as their own context changes.

You may wish to consider the mechanisms by which power is held. Can you 'take' power from someone, or simply make them believe that they have lost it?

> • **Have you ever tried to exert power only to discover that the battery is flat?**

It seems likely that power can be considered in both relative and absolute terms. Absolute power is quantified, visible, codified, and written for all to see (like your job title or role description), while other power can be relative to those around you. We all have a reputation, but yours may, in context, be stronger than mine.

Power may also be viewed in terms of belief. If I 'believe' that you are powerful, the chances are that this makes you so.

Similarly, if I lack belief in you, then you may be powerless, possibly even if your contract tells you the opposite.

Our power can be subverted, bypassed, or undermined in many simple ways.

I remember reading of a group who sought to subvert the activity of a power company by overpaying their monthly bills by one cent. This triggered a refund process that took time, cost money, and added complexity to the power company's workload. By doing more of what was permitted, they drained power, or gained influence. Or to put it another way, they got themselves noticed.

11.

WHAT CAN YOU DEMAND?

Your power allows you to demand certain things: your attendance, your conformity, your input, your money, your time, and your skill, for example.

There are other things you cannot demand, or are unlikely to get, whatever power you hold: your belief, your trust, your certainty, your vulnerability, and your hope, for instance.

Some things can be bought, and others only invested in.

If we are lucky, we may gain additional items at no cost. I may buy your time, act with integrity, or earn your trust.

Conversely, I may buy your time, abuse your trust, and earn your doubt or fear.

While we can demand some things, the act of demanding may erode the very thing we seek. I may demand your belief, but by doing so expose the weakness of my work. Alternatively, I may demand your loyalty, but by doing so make you realise that I hold no loyalty from others.

Some things it may be possible, but wrong, for us to demand.

To demand some things may come at the cost of our integrity or authenticity. This is a particular challenge in times of change.

- What can you demand, and what should you demand? What can never be demanded?

- What is the cost of demanding, as opposed to asking for something or earning it?

- At what point is demanding an act of desperation? Conversely, when is it right to demand?

- Is it fair to demand and expect honesty in return? Is it fair to demand punctuality or reliability?

- Is it right and fair to demand your best effort?

12.

WHAT HAS BEEN GIVEN TO YOU?

Aside from your laptop and phone, what has been given to you?

Organisations often gift assets: hardware, space, badges, and uniforms, for example.

As well as these things, they sometimes gift access: specifically, permissions and passes that grant access to spaces and resources.

- Have you been given opportunities, space, belief, resources, and time?
- Have you been given a place to belong?

Belonging is one of the most interesting aspects of a Socially Dynamic Organisation, not because it is contracted or demanded, but because it is earned.

- Do we give people space to belong, or a key to the door, or a rulebook, or a process to follow?
- Have you been given the trust of others, or the keys to the store cupboard?
- Have you got the company credit card, or the ability to sign things off?
- Have you been given the power to punish others, or to hold them to account? Have you been given the power to simply see or hear in privileged spaces?
- Indeed, have you been given privilege itself, through gender, ancestry, geography, sponsorship, or something else?

When you think about what has been given to you, consider what you can give to others?

Do you have a responsibility, moral or otherwise, to do so?

THE FRAGILITY OF YOUR POWER

Just as no power is infinite in reach, so too no power is permanent in application. Power is fragile, sometimes alarmingly so, sometimes surprisingly so.

As power is held in reputation as well as hierarchy and structure, it is changeable. This fragility can lead us to defend existing power, or hold back from necessary action.

In this, our fourth and final section, we will consider a further four questions, exploring how our power may be fragile. We will think about uncertainty, doubt, fear, and the consequences of fragile power, and additionally how these things steer, limit, and shape our actions.

© Julian Stodd

13.

WHAT ARE YOU UNCERTAIN ABOUT?

It is easy to fall into the trap of believing that our strength lies in our certainty, and that our certainty gives us power.

Sometimes this is true, but even if only to be true to ourselves, we should actively consider where our uncertainty lies.

- How do you hold uncertainty? Inside, or in conversation? In public, in certain communities, or with trusted partners?

- How has your uncertainty been used against you? Or, conversely, have you ever felt that your own uncertainty has created space or opportunity for others, or even created loyalty or engagement?

- Are you uncertain about things that you 'should know already', or new things that you 'should learn to know'? Essentially, is your uncertainty forward - or legacy - facing?

- Do you ever fear being 'found out', and does this sense of being an imposter, or a fake, have any basis in reality?

- How is uncertainty transmitted and shared?

- If you are uncertain, does it give others the space to be so too? Is that a good thing or a weakness for an Organisation?

- Can uncertainty be an opportunity, is it always a risk, or does it depend? If so...on what?

- Are there things that you have been certain about for a long time, but that now you feel doubtful about? If so, is that a good or a bad thing?

- Is uncertainty a foundation for learning, or for change?

- Can you change without uncertainty?

- Does uncertainty make you weaker or stronger as a leader? How do you judge it in others?

- Does your judgement depend upon whether you like or respect somebody already?

14.

HOW DO YOU CARRY DOUBT?

Doubt, which is related to uncertainty, should be considered in all its forms. These include self-doubt, righteous doubt, doubt about rules and systems, and doubt about the actions of others.

GRAFFITI SPACE

- Is a healthy cynicism a crucial aspect of leadership?

- Do you carry doubt out as curiosity and/or fear, close to your chest, or at arm's length?

- How do you hear the doubt that others carry? Do you have to ask to hear it, or is it on view if you are willing to look or listen?

- Do you have access to the spaces where doubt is shared? Does everyone hold the same type of doubt, or does it vary?

- What is the price of doubt, for you or others around you?

- Can your doubt impose a cost on others?

15.

WHAT DO YOU FEAR?

Fear is a powerful force. It can limit or silence some people, while empowering and motivating others.

Fear, like other social currencies, is traded within our communities. It can be gifted or imposed, transient or permanent, and is always highly contextual.

Fear may act as an amplifier, or brake, upon our power. To therefore understand what our fears are, and how fear affects us, is valuable.

- **What are you afraid of?**

At two years old, my son is developing fear. Learning to be fearful of strangers, of monsters under the bed, of how others judge us, and of being laughed at when in the wrong, is a natural part of life.

In some ways, fear is a loss of innocence. Yet fear is not simply a bad or negative thing.

Fear keeps us safe. Fear of being burned stops us touching the fire on the gas cooker, just as fear of being excluded may encourage us to resolve conflicts and find common ground.

Fear of being left behind may motivate us to learn, while fear of others being left behind may motivate us to share.

Equally, fear may be used as a weapon that is imposed upon others, or controls or influences them. Fear can rob us of our energy and freedom. It can stifle our imagination.

Fear of being ordinary or average can motivate us to go further in life. Fear of failure, on the other hand, may cause us to work late and get ahead, although possibly at the expense of our friendships and family life.

The cost of fear may not be borne by us directly, but rather by those who care for us.

Our power may be fragile because of our own and others' fear.

If we view power as belief, then fear may damage others' ability to believe. If we view it as structure, then fear of loss, of position, or of membership, may cause us to stay silent when we should speak up.

16.

HOW DO YOU EXPERIENCE CONSEQUENCE?

When we reach too far, we experience consequence. It's an inherent feature of both formal and social systems. If we transgress a rule, written or implicit, we may be reprimanded, penalised, or excluded.

Our understanding of the reach, limits, action, and fairness of consequence, as well as the mechanisms through which it is judged and applied, may make our power fragile.

- In your own work, how do you experience consequence?

- Through the overt judgement of others? Through stories? Through comments? Through impacts? Through loss?

- Is it always clear by which rules consequence is applied?

- Does it sometimes fall out of the sky, with no warning, or is the pathway to consequence always clear?

I've written elsewhere about the Sphere of Consequence. This work views consequence as coming in two forms: that which is imposed, and that which we impose upon ourselves.

Our experience of externally imposed consequence may cause us to recoil or draw back from situations. Essentially, we create an insulation gap between the pain we have felt, and the pain we fear. We therefore end up limiting ourselves to keep ourselves safe.

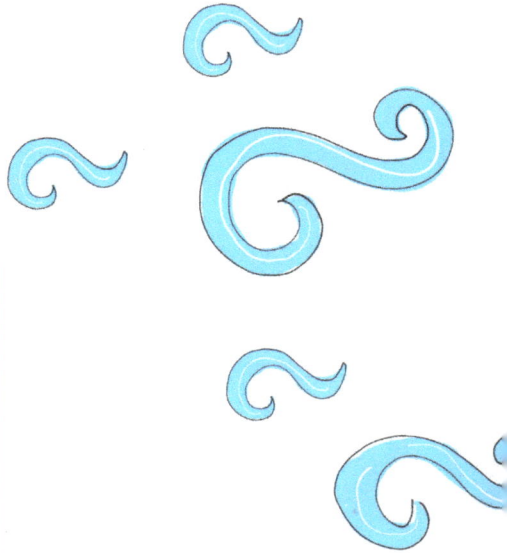

- How do you apply consequence? How do you govern the limits of consequence?

- How do you ensure that consequence flows fairly, and is there a way to withdraw it?

- How does consequence make our power fragile? Is it through absolute limits and making us scared to use our power to the fullest?

YOUR POWER

Through these 16 questions, we have walked through the landscape of our own power.

I hope that you have found some things comforting, and others challenging.

Our power is not fixed. Some power can slip away from us, while other power may be found as our context changes.

Our relationship with power should, rightly, be reflective: that which we take for granted may hurt us the most when it is lost.

With the shape you have drawn, perhaps you can see opportunity, or perhaps you merely feel comfort.

Either is fine.

We may have everything we need already, or we may lack a full view of our potential.

Leadership is, itself, an exploratory act, one which moves from learning and reflection into practice, and back again.

These questions may help us complete those cycles of thinking, sense-making, doing, reflecting, learning, planning, and so on.

YOUR POTENTIAL

Where we end up is just the start.

Exploring power is not diagnostic. It does not, in itself, tell us what we need, but it may make us more aware of what we already have, or have access to.

Your potential may lie through being consistent in how you already lead, or in the evolution of your leadership.

However, not every change is additive: you cannot do everything.

Perhaps you need to leave some things behind, or to stop doing them.

It's easy to stare ahead and think of your perfect future self, but ask what weight you can carry on the journey to become that person.

Perhaps our last action, as we explore the power and potential of our leadership, should be to ask ourselves a final question.

What can you leave behind?

Potential is not simply an empty space waiting to be filled, but rather a dynamic story waiting to be written and engaged with.

Your own potential as a leader is tied up with the potential of the system you inhabit as well: a dynamic interplay between formal and social structures, between self and system.

FURTHER READING

THE GUIDEBOOK SERIES

I've written a series of *'Guidebooks'* for the Social Age: these cover aspects of my work that are still rapidly evolving, or which I have not made time to write a full book about yet. They are typically under 10k words, and are intended to provide an overview of the landscape. I try to keep them practical, with a key highlight on *'what you need to know'*, and *'what you can do about it'*.

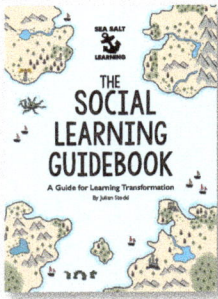

The Social Learning Guidebook

Provides a practical overview for the principles and design techniques of Social Learning in a modern organisation.

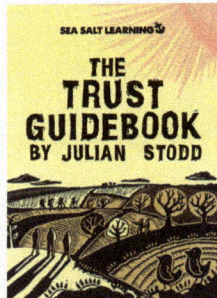

The Trust Guidebook

Explores our extensive research into the Landscape of Trust, and asks 72 questions that leaders can use with their teams.

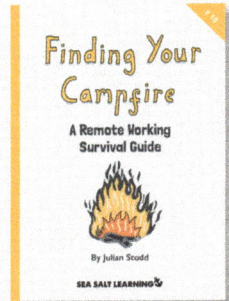

Finding Your Campfire

This short book is a survival guide for individuals, teams, and organisations navigating the experience of remote work.

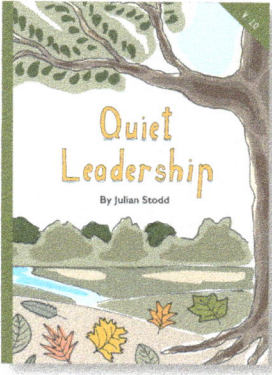

Quiet Leadership considers the Organisations that we inhabit as an ecosystem, and the way that none of us can tend to the whole of this system alone. Only by connecting at the most local level, through the smallest of actions, can we weave a strength into our culture, and keep the ecosystem healthy at scale.

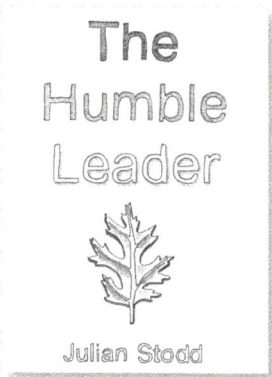

The Humble Leader is a guided reflection into our personal humility as a Social Leader.

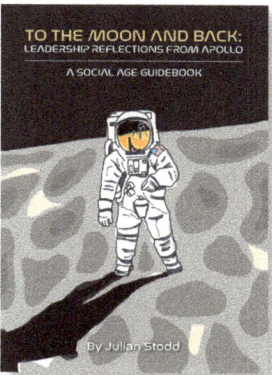

To the Moon and Back: Leadership Reflections from Apollo shares eight key stories about the Apollo programme, alongside my personal reflection on what this means for Leadership in the Social Age.

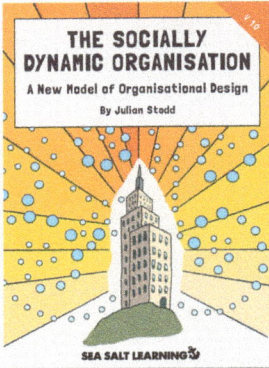

The Socially Dynamic Organisation
For a new type of world, we will need a new type of Organisation: one that is lightweight and rapidly adaptable, that thrives in times of constant change, that respects the old but embraces the new.

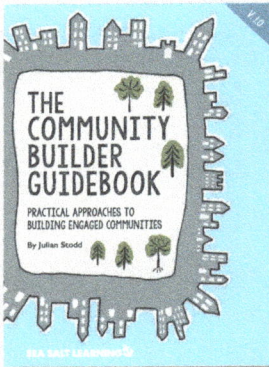

The Community Builder Guidebook brings you practical ideas to create engaged and dynamic Social Learning Communities and Communities of Practice.

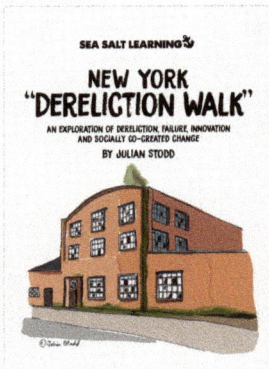

The New York Dereliction Walk is more experimental work, exploring how Organisations and ideas fall derelict and fail, but can be reborn through social movements. It was my favourite writing from 2018.

THE HANDBOOK SERIES

'Handbooks' are intended to capture a full snapshot of my evolving body of work on a particular subject. *'The Social Leadership Handbook'*, now in its second edition, explores the intersection of Formal and Social authority, and considers the importance of this in the context of the Social Age.

I'm currently finishing writing *'The Change Handbook'*, which is an exploration of how Organisations change, and the forces that hold them constrained. It considers how we build more Socially Dynamic Organisations.

THE '100 DAY', & 'SKETCHBOOK', SERIES

Whilst *'Handbooks'* and *'Guidebooks'* are about ideas and strategy, the *'100 Day'* books tackle how we do these things at scale. They do so by providing a scaffolded space, which you can explore, document, and graffiti, as you go.

'Social Leadership: My First 100 Days' is a practical, guided, reflective journey. It follows 100 days of activity, with each day including provocations, questions, and actions. You fill in the book as you go. It's accompanied by a full set of 100 podcasts.

'The Trust Sketchbook' is another guided, reflective journey, a walk through the Landscape of Trust, but in this case you graffiti and adapt the book, to capture your own landscape.

OTHER BOOKS

I have written a series of other books, covering aspects of learning, culture technology, and knowledge, which you can find details of on the blog.

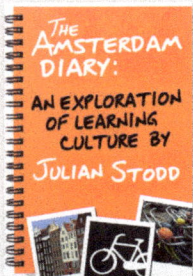

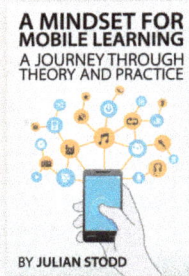

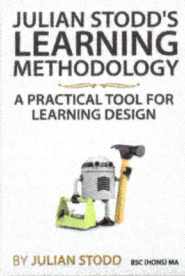

CERTIFICATIONS

In 2018 I launched the first Certification programme on *'Storytelling in Social Leadership'*. It's based upon *'Foundations'* and *'Techniques'*, which are practical and applied, and *'Experiments'*, which you learn to run in your own Organisation.

'Storytelling in Social Leadership'

'Leading with Trust'

'Community Building'

'Foundations of Social Leadership'

'Modern Learning Capabilities'

'Leading Through Change'

'Social Age Navigation'

Get in touch to find out more
www.seasaltlearning.com/certifications

SOCIAL LEADERSHIP DAILY

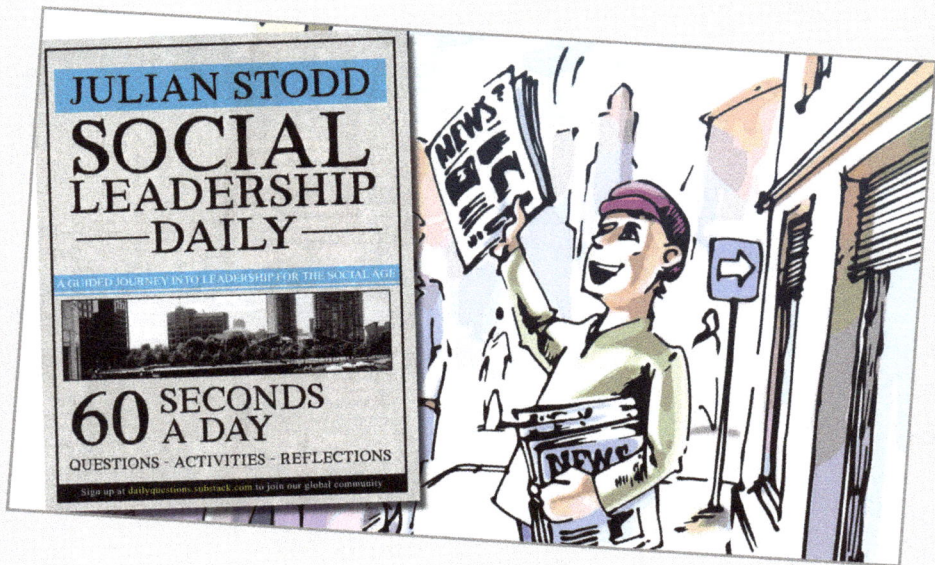

Daily questions, activities, and reflection in the arms of a global community of Explorers, putting Social Leadership into their everyday practice.

dailyquestions.substack.com

ABOUT SEA SALT LEARNING

We are a dynamic *Social Age startup:* living the values we speak. We are virtualised, global, inclusive, and agile. We are a core team of around twenty Crew Mates.

We are surrounded by a much larger layer of Social Age *'Explorers'*, people who are heavily involved in *'sense making'* around our core topics of Social Learning, Social Leadership, Change, Culture, and the Socially Dynamic Organisation.

Sea Salt Learning builds upon the work by Julian Stodd, author and explorer of the Social Age, recognised for his pioneering work in helping organisations to adapt to the new reality of the Social Age.

The **Sea Salt Research Hub** carries out original, creative, and large scale research, providing an evidence base for our work.

Sea Salt Publishing provides a curated body of books and online publications, exploring all aspects of the Social Age.

Sea Salt Digital provides our technical capability and build capacity for eLearning, mobile, video, and other forms of online learning.

GETTING IN CONTACT

Find out more about how our Guidebooks can help you and your Organisation.

If you want to discuss any of the products in this Guidebook, or discuss your particular requirements, you can reach us here:

Talk to us: hello@seasaltlearning.com

Website: seasaltlearning.com

Find us on twitter: @seasaltlearning

Julian's blog: julianstodd.wordpress.com

Julian's twitter: @julianstodd

©Julian Stodd

www.ingramcontent.com/pod-product-compliance
Lightning Source LLC
Chambersburg PA
CBHW040930210326
41597CB00030B/5254